LEARN
SCISSOR SKILLS!

PETER PAUPER PRESS, INC.

White Plains, New York

PETER PAUPER PRESS

In 1928, at the age of twenty-two, Peter Beilenson began printing books on a small press in the basement of his parents' home in Larchmont, New York. Peter—and later, his wife, Edna—sought to create fine books that sold at "prices even a pauper could afford."

Today, still family owned and operated, Peter Pauper Press continues to honor our founders' legacy of quality, value, and fun for big kids and small kids alike.

Illustrations copyright © 2019 Martha Day Zschock
Designed by Heather Zschock

Copyright © 2019
Peter Pauper Press, Inc.
Manufactured for Peter Pauper Press, Inc.
202 Mamaroneck Avenue
White Plains, NY 10601 USA
All rights reserved
ISBN 978-1-4413-3113-7
Printed in China

Published in the United Kingdom and Europe by
Peter Pauper Press, Inc. c/o White Pebble International
Unit 2, Plot 11 Terminus Road
Chichester, West Sussex PO19 8TX, UK

7 6 5

Visit us at www.peterpauper.com

This book will help your child learn how to use scissors. It features simple puzzles, shapes, and fun projects to cut out and glue together. The safety scissors included will give your child the confidence and practice he or she needs to perfect their scissor proficiency and develop fine motor skills.

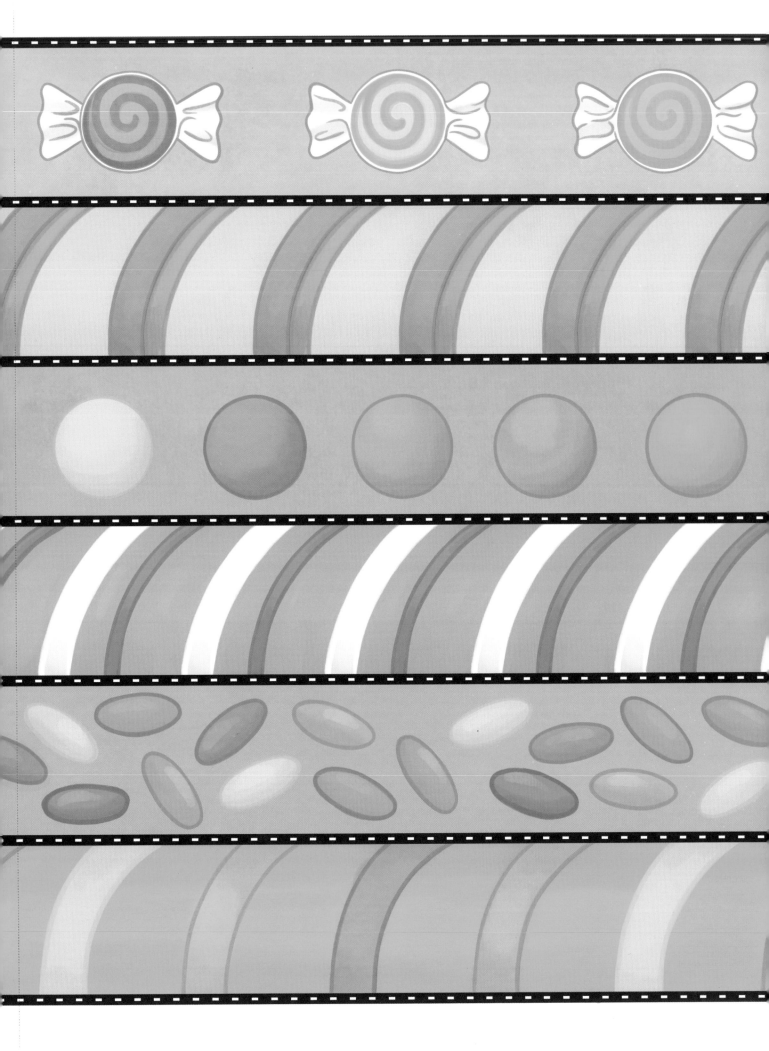

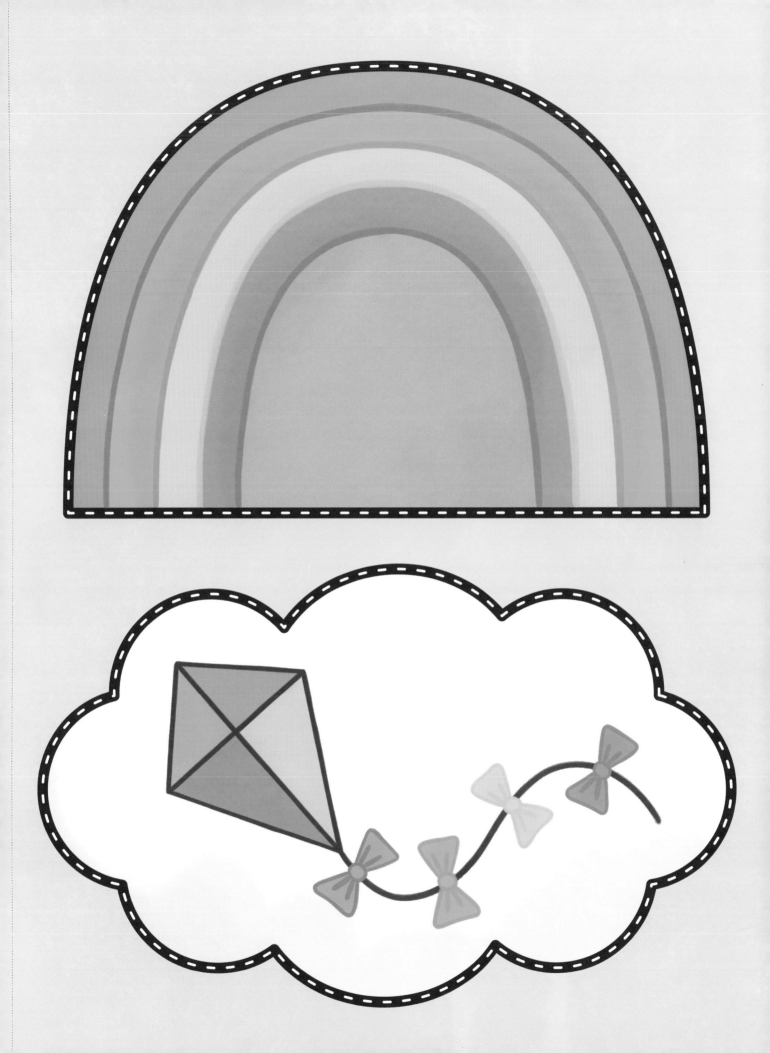

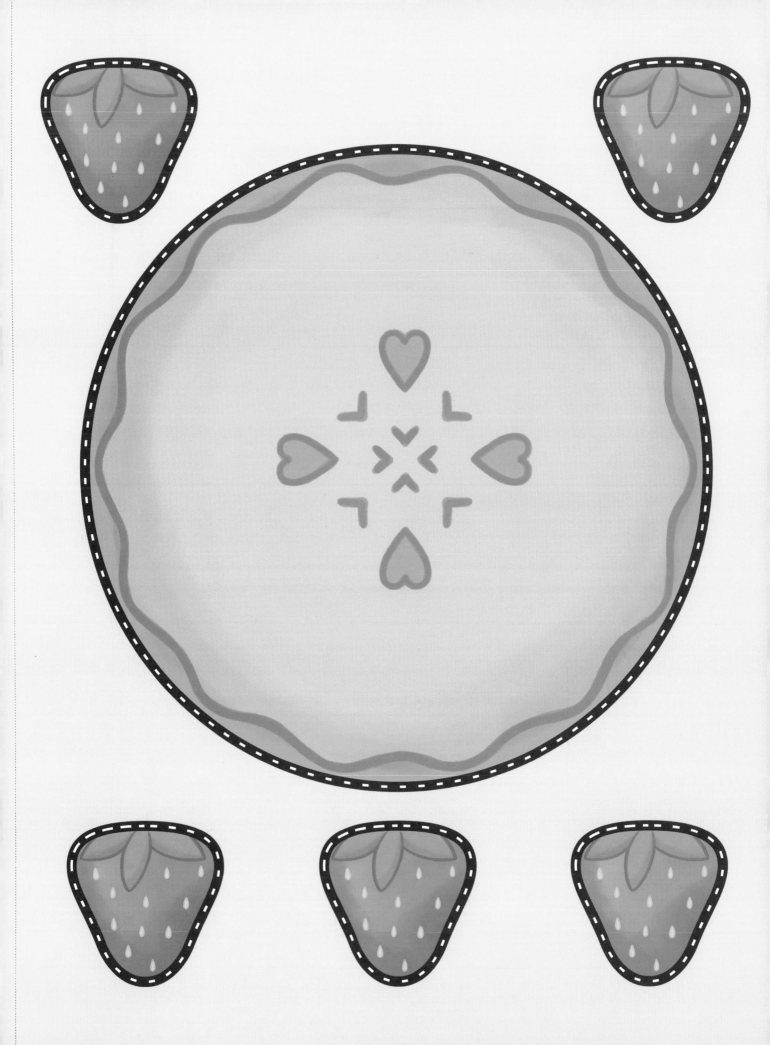

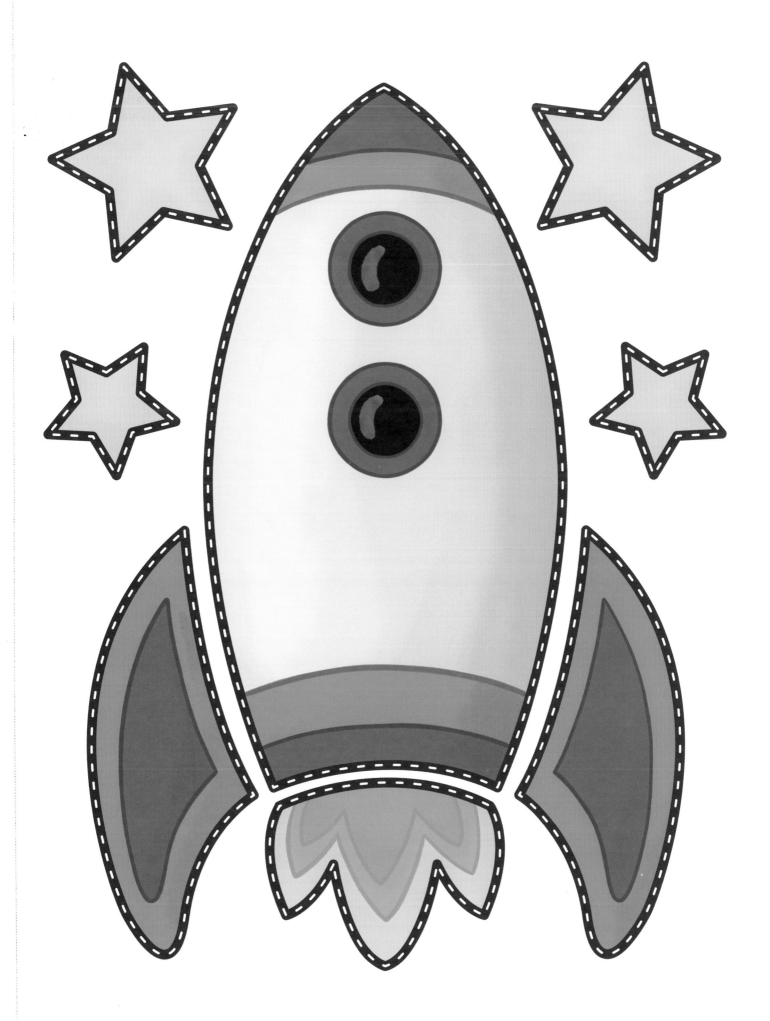

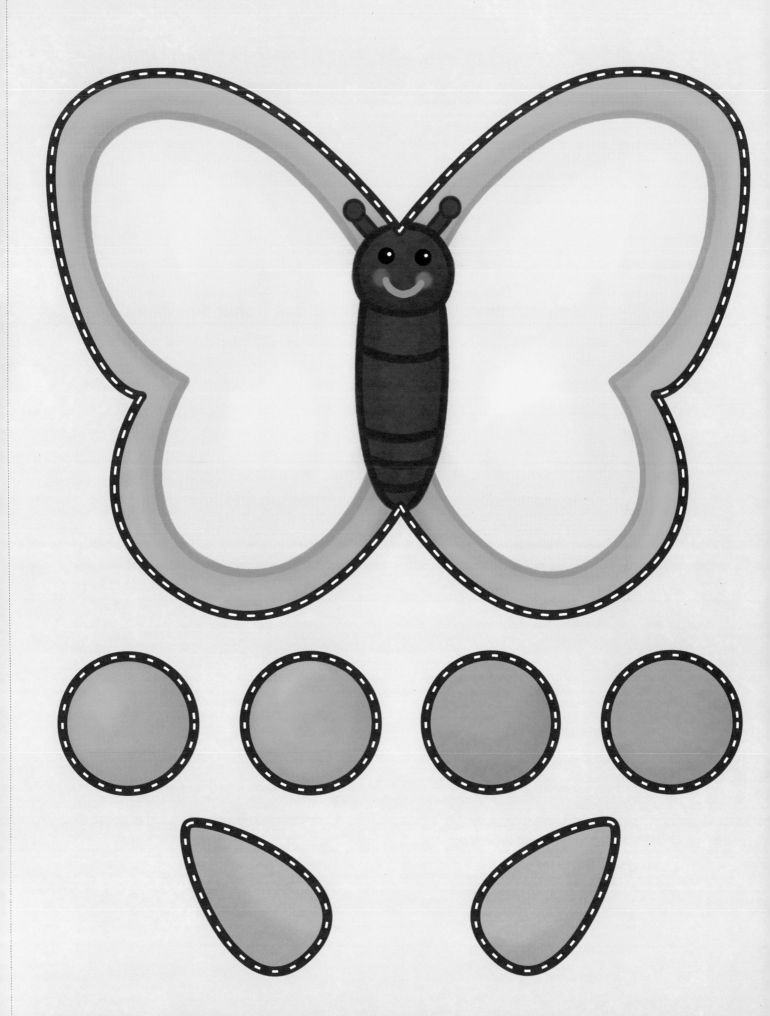

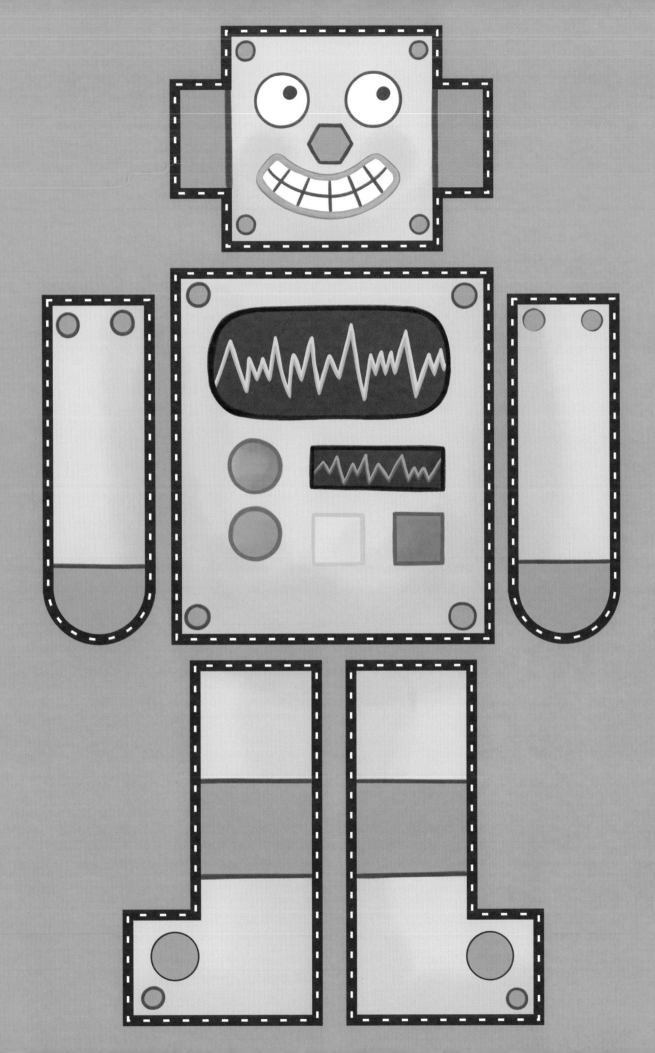

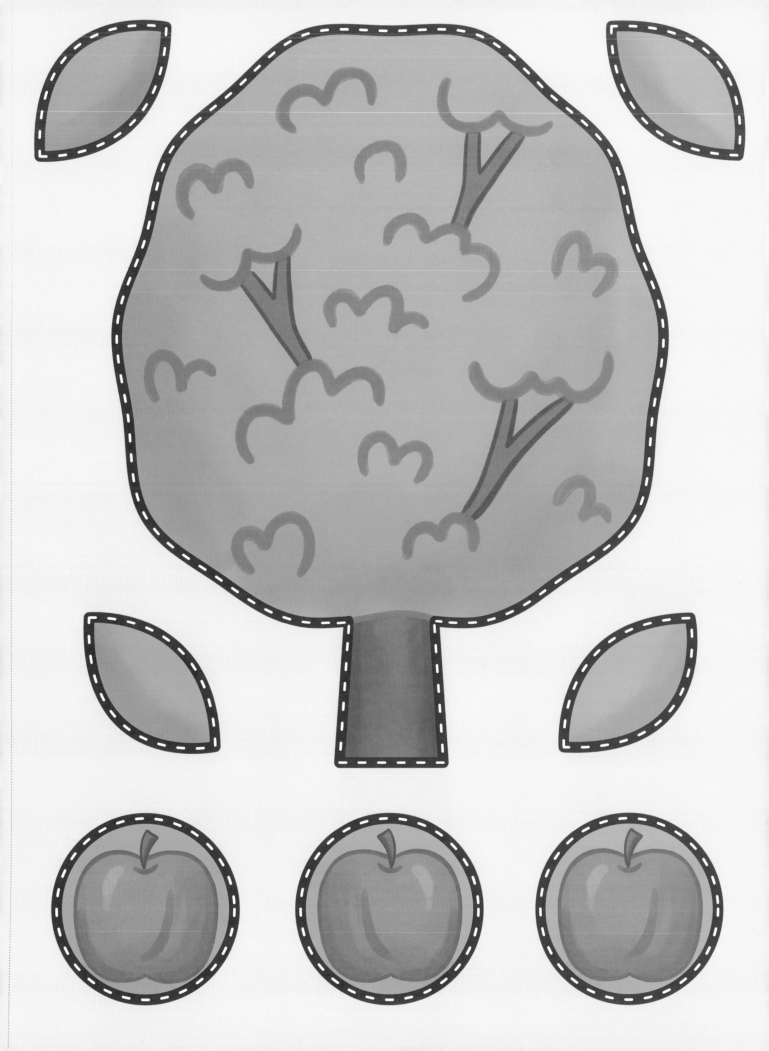

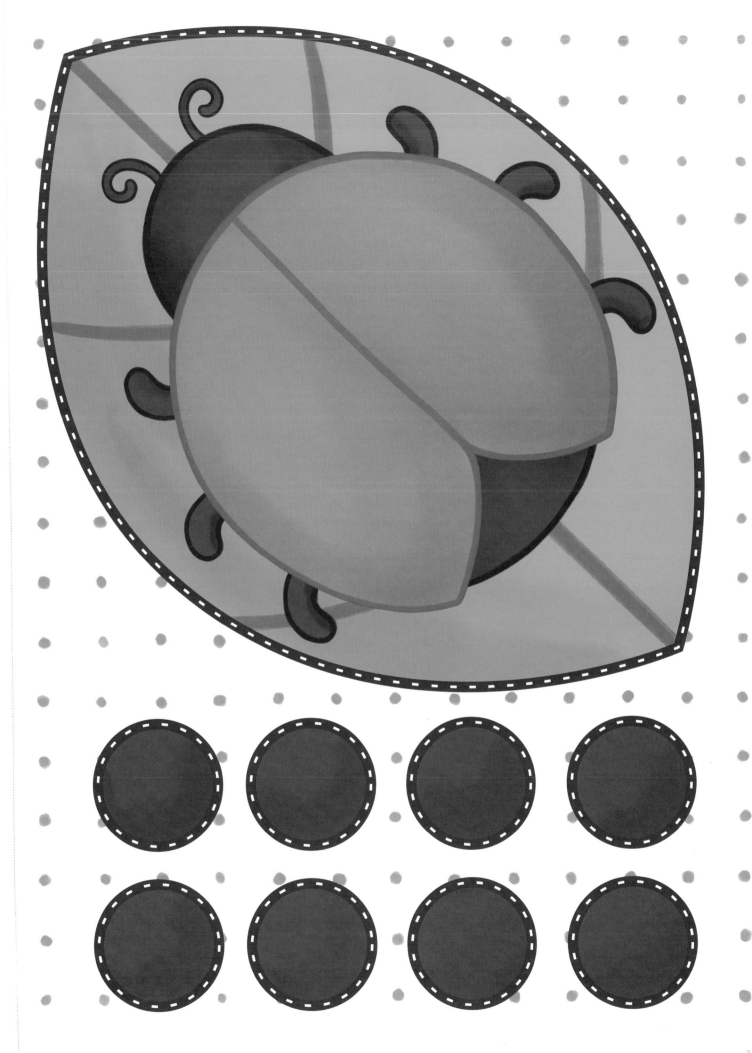

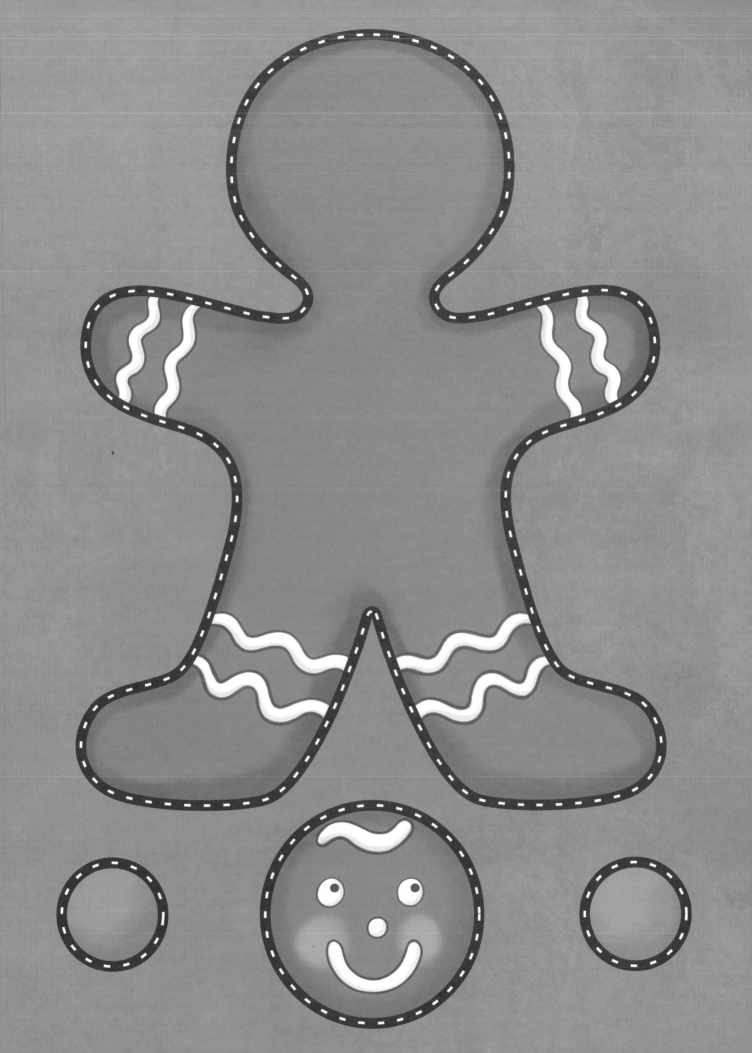